ALEXANDRIA

ALEXANDRIA

Jasmine V. Bailey

Carnegie Mellon University Press
Pittsburgh 2014

ACKNOWLEDGMENTS

The author wishes to thank the following journals and chapbook in which versions of these poems appear:

32 Poems: "Archipelago"
Bat Terrier Review: "Wildwood"
Bayou Magazine: "Alexandria"
Birmingham Poetry Review: "Six Years On," "Concerning Gorky's *The Artist and His Mother*"
Buddhist Poetry Review: "After Ryokan," "Preparing to Leave Virginia," "Hiking the Lake Placid Trail"
Hayden's Ferry Review: "Migration"
Inch: "Sometime Galatea," "Calligraphy"
Indigo Rising: "Bonsai," "Boarding School," "The Middle Kingdom," "Santa Rosa, La Pampa," "For a Tall Man," "Morse"
the minnesota review: "Charon"
Slushpile: "Days of Aggressive Geese" (formerly "October Flowers")
South Dakota Review: "Woodcutter," "Dendrology," "Coalescence"

Sleep and What Precedes It, Longleaf Press: "Poem after Summer," "Sleep and What Precedes It," "Two Autumns," "Days of Aggressive Geese," "Dreaming in January," and "For Helen"

Book design by Lou Lamanna

10 9 8 7 6 5 4 3 2 1

for Richard X. Bailey
& Linda A. Bailey

It stays there for the rest of your life, unspoken,
made of that dirt we call earth, the metal we call salt,
in a form we have no words for, and you live on it.

—Philip Levine

CONTENTS

Part One

Part Two

Part Three

As one long prepared and graced with courage,
as is right for you who were given this kind of city,
go firmly to the window
and listen with deep emotion, but not
with the whining, the pleas of a coward;
listen—your final delectation—to the voices,
to the exquisite music of that strange procession,
and say goodbye to her, to the Alexandria you are losing.

—Constantine P. Cavafy

Part One

ARCHIPELAGO

You have come into and out of my life
like a needle knitting me to the earth.
Here and not here, rising and diving.

Yours is a love that requires
talking to sounds that gather in grass,
holding a bottle by the neck. Why blame you

for the end of summer or its reprisal?
Why march down to the road
and travel it? I don't know. We must accept

everything. Light seems to exist just for us
and still the mushrooms after the last rain
are all suspicious.

It has taken a long time to accept
the fall of twilight into evening,
my perpetual dinner of roses.

POEM AFTER SUMMER

If I created a world I would call it Virginia every so often
it would rain. You and I would set decoys out on the lakes
where they would float among the pinprick raindrops. Evenings,
we would bring them in and scatter the geese from their flirting.
We would understand everything about fall, where it wanders,
why the saddest books are always turned to then, the oldest poems.
We would know why haikus arrange themselves in little lines,
why waltzes begin again at four, realize that to die is to forget
the world and that all the heroes forgot us. We would set about
forgetting peaches, knowing that is the best place to begin.

SUGAR HOLLOW

Tally the damages of our parting this way:
go to a swimming hole and take off your clothes.

Do this because I want to imagine you
breasting the cold water,

moving towards a fallen branch,
clutching it as you submerge.

Small fish will forget you
and dart around your ankles, a turtle will sleep

on the same log you sun yourself on,
out of reach.

You will not deify, you will not
alchemize—

you were already a god and gold;
I was there for it.

The mosquito net drawn around us,
time gave up freckling our bodies; I could see

you only, lit and dim.
In my mind you have always just finished

a handful of berries.

BONSAI

To have had a good man and lost him, for any reason—
is to recover slowly from it, if at all. The world
offers up few consolations and too easily each day
can seem a barrenness. She thinks back on him—
was he ever there? The same trees grope at the sky,
the same wasps spin in the oak, the gravel collects,
and the hummingbird sips nectar on the other side
of its feeder. Give me a little strange light or air
of the ensuing season. Let a leaf feather through branches
for a quarter of an hour before it lands in still summer.
Show me a reflection of the vessel we rise out of.

Sleep and What Precedes It

I had a vantage of your body once, as from a great height
though I was just lifting my chin.

This afternoon made my hair soft and the light
came through the window onto me.

This is how Ashley and I slept in college, afternoons
beneath bay windows. I suspect

that's where I grew my extent of lovely,
my pint of summer raspberries:

in the sun and her proximity.
I know I was different when it was over.

I dig my fingers into your hair and you lift your chin
as if balancing an imaginary cup of tea

or something consequential, like the fate of American beef.
There is something there that must not spill.

There is a child of thought I have not
made leap from the pond in you

that lies dusted with leaves.
How do things happen? Where does the energy come from

to make us light enough to float
into each other?

I looked at you last night, relieved
for a time of my desire, and you were beautiful.

Morse

I have seen deer appear and disappear
in the forest near my house. Some are born
looking, some with their mouths in grass.
Almost nothing moves like deer, without lines.
Night is when the last eye vanishes
and the cicadas emerge, all voice.
If we go on like this too long, we will also win
our long night of messages.

SHAMROCK ROAD

Even now the shade of your tulip tree
this second bad August of ours is a lance
to some balloon I ride through my life.
If I could survive on ground, sit through
your film noir, we'd have the drawer

you quoted of underthings
tangled together. Who dreamed
this passion or the next one, who
the new infertility of a place not changed?
When evening again picks up
its conversation, I will look everywhere
for things that are not mad.

THE MIDDLE KINGDOM

Your preserved body
bound to its gifts—was it I
who wrapped you

in linen, who arranged
the slaves
in their many little boats?

Turquoise and porphyry
weigh you to a stone,
pomegranates

oversweeten your breath.
And I am not satisfied
I'll find you here again,

or grave-robbed, or departed
to the golden afterlife.

BOARDING SCHOOL

Owlets were moored in the distant tree.
Your down, your well-tended geese
and lambs that never grew.

You are where I have buried
the empty opera house
and whole forests. You I opened

like our clothes
to the wind's lunatic freedoms.
The clarinet it made of the merest Wednesday.

Perhaps you already knew
that no one can live
without disturbing the leaves.

FOR A TALL MAN

Not easy to remember old lovers
the mind has worn down like a coast—
what the inside of his wrist was,
how the ginkgos met over us some night
in yellow-green applause.

I've forgotten one who I once believed
would be my children's father.
Such bravado of a young woman—
each untried detail of herself insoluble.

THE STRENGTH OF YOUNG
MEN TO THROW THINGS

There was something of us that was the same—
I recognized in his fingers, his studies, his toilette,
aspects of the unperfectable.
He could never get past me in love
to turn back and hold out a hand.

He made omelets and gave me a rose or two,
stealing the ingredients and the roses.
I was going mad at that time, but
it was he who broke down first:
tomatoes, oil and flowers cast
desperately like rice on the Chenango.

VAL DE LOIRE

In the performance of his madness
as well as his madness, much good theater:
the dramatic kiss he gave his rival,
countless grave appearances with the entourage
of a single Persian woman.

I don't think I could inspire that anymore—
we were like people going blind,
looking harder at one poppy
than a painter driving through France
looks at the teeming orange fields.

STAR OF DAVID

It's true I've often left,
but never with your elegance—
tall, sad, carrying the one real kiss.
Who slept as perfectly in a heap of cans
or climbed the ski hill so sincerely?

You were lean as a smile,
slicing cucumbers, wilting lettuce,
folding jokes into your pocket—
your Star of David on my lips
or caught in hair.

After each blanket in the muddy town
has been washed and our footsteps
smoothed by runoff, your beauty catches
in my throat and I hunger after
forgiveness.

CANARY

I used you as a pawn to chip sideways
at a lost game. A slow, senseless march
down the board while the better player
arranged my loss.

Painfully I revealed myself to you—
the yellow dress, the Italian restaurant,
up to certain impassable points.

I made the requisite sacrifices—
I endured your parents.
But I never threw myself from a cliff
as I used to say I would.

How that excited you.

SOMETIME GALATEA

I've seen the way some statues rest,
like they've made love so hard
they'll never wake up.

To wish to be beautiful is
to misunderstand
how it removes you from the world.

Then again, how not to wish for it,
even knowing that, when he turns,
it vanishes.

MY VIARDOT

Tonight wood smoke empties
into the fog for us to smell.
In Lebanon the sky undresses
and we don't honor the fathomless
by looking at the stars for order,
unsnapping the superfluous jacket,
pulling the zipper of the fleece,
finding the hair on the flat
truth of the sternum,
and marking its elevation with the tongue.
I should count the gray strands
in your hair from between my fingers.
Animals should start
at our screams. Something names this
other than love, something so remote
it can be obeyed but not believed.
Your body goes to Russia,
the dream of my hands still clutching it.

EVIDENCE OF AUTUMN

No end to the appetite
of a love such as the one I felt for you.
A year was so little substance,
its few thin evenings,
one trip abroad like a strip of floss.

The orphan god
stomps through heaven demanding goats.
This is all the proof we get of infinity:
the conviction he can eat forever.

Part Two

Migration

Summer leaves for South America
taking heat and hummingbirds
and the last good tomato.

I asked for inevitable changes
because I wanted gratification and because
the lavender plant would not grow—

the whole damn garden
was a failure. I would like to go south
to look for green violetears

and where my ruby throat
is wintering.
The day I left for Argentina,

moonlight found its way
into the airport,
and I became a lake.

EMPRESS, CONCUBINE

From the mess of the nightstand,
a chrysanthemum. No onlooker
to resent or illumine its beauty.
This quiet is the life to accept
as yours—even the bugs have shut down
in the October cold and you want
with nowhere to place it except holes
dug in the ground with a broken shovel.

No one examines what evening does to one
alone in the perfect autumn quiet.
Bring your wrong love and your one
bottle of whiskey. We will drink it
all the way out of the wizened city
back to where each other's presence
has confused us from.

CALLIGRAPHY

The amaryllis grows into a long, green sickle
the shade holds up. To be made useful,
elegant this way, supporting the weight
of something grown beyond its control.

To be the window that frames this, on one side
the shade and leaf, on the other the theater of trees.
To be a place where two worlds never cease
looking at each other.

Two Autumns

I am the plant in soil,
the cutting in water,
dew, a typhoon, the eastern shore.

I am the one who takes down,
in shorthand, millennia
of cedar trees, their quiet cataclysms,

their dry sufferings.
I do not move,
but maybe I move.

After all I've moved before
in my still way.
I've transferred

dreams and nightmares
to new rooms where
they hung like piñatas from the eaves.

I am the nerves of the human
organism, I shudder and ache.
I seize and retract.

I am the infinite one,
but maybe I end. Maybe
we walk away in careless radii

or like the French guessed,
there is no center to the universe.
Perhaps there are more autumns

than merely
the one that litters you with leaves,
without me.

Apologia

The fog of going so long unfavored—
how to emerge? I beat myself
against you just shy of murder
then sat with my hand parallel
to the surface of a pool, almost touching it.

Imagine a man like that—such hair,
such limbs—the mists evaporating.
His red shorts caught my eye
and then my vision skated over the lengths of him,
brushing everything with goldenrod.
My face at that time was
a hieroglyph not yet deciphered.
European starlings bickered in the trees;
it was the right month for cava.

Wildwood

I required wine
and you brought two bottles to the beach,
where I undressed you

the common way—imagining it.
You lodged yourself
in the way of some fantasies,

blocking my view of the north side of Paris.
You were the color of almonds

almost burnt in a dry pan,
but you could not rival Paris.

AFTER SARATOGA

One afternoon of apple picking
then back to your careless house
for kofta and a new release.

I managed to assemble a pie,
then gave up on plenty
and apples.

Dancing waters in the pool,
precarious ledges,
the Egg—our study

of Albany's engineering.
I began and ended the same:
too poor for you

or the next man who arrived,
his pockets spilling
vanilla cigarettes.

The Eumenides

Hard to say whether my scale tilted
towards the blessings or the curses—
only misery and humble memories
fight for privilege in these hours.

It is not unreasonable to say you were
the way a god is: adored, jealous. One
could say you were my god. But when
does anyone clamor to talk of us?

Where has the panel gathered, those
come forth to sort out, for once and for all,
which of us will finally leave in flight,
and which will inherit Athens?

DAYS OF AGGRESSIVE GEESE

On our bridge in Firenze, in the painting,
in the Renaissance, that cream morning,
sometimes you were Dante and sometimes
you were Beatrice. Sometimes I was the river,
sometimes the loose woman, and sometimes
we were both the blue friend looking on with
that unsettling face of discernment. Sometimes
I held a flower, gazing after my mother's window,
sometimes you put a foot out and held your heart.
Sometimes you held the violet and I my heart.

•

There were the people of God and the people
of drink and we were the people who wanted
to make Virginia like a winter jasmine open
in them. We stepped into your yard in slippers
and found a daffodil that meant to be itself in
a new way, to burst out of its own beauty into
another beauty. It was a loved thing, or at least
the consequence of a loved thing, as our gestures,
our pictures with the tulips, our showers, our weekdays,
had the color and scent and dew of loved things.

Champlain

The swan's perfect angles
are safer in art, indoors,
free from lice and the search
for cress. But I want to release
the two above my bookshelf
into the lake at night
when cold has seized
the water in the air
and veiled the sleeping geese.
Their feet unfold the way
arms emerge from a sweater
and the whole chest
is a secret that magnifies
in darkness. The more naked
you become, the vaster
the territory you illumine—
our wrists and knees
are eloquent in the variations
of alphabet. Your arms
spell ocean, my back
writes winter.

DELPHI

Before all the olive trees go extinct,
you will have gone. I cannot convince you
there is only one loss,
but I think you will know it.
You've already seen a small forest
cleared for quick sale.

I do not know everything—who and how
you loved in the final tally. I know
what the trees in front of me are doing.
When I go to town, I know
what the couple at the table next to me
is quoting—an old movie.

And I know there's one loss
travelling the continents like a glamorous actress.
At each last wonder she can be seen
sipping espresso, looking at nothing.
She fools some people with her sunglasses,
always changing her name.

Santa Rosa, La Pampa

When my parents got into the taxi
to leave Argentina, to leave me
in Argentina, I couldn't wait for them
to pull away to begin crying.
Five months more alone
in the hemisphere. Time
in my town of rusted cars.
I don't know what you would've done
or what street I stood on.
Someone said, consolingly,
It's always harder to stay behind.
It was that beautiful a country.

WOODCUTTER

The loneliness of the man who stacks
half a cord in the shed
quiets my monologue.

In his stories a dead wife and mother,
a witless father and a brother
toothless from seizures.

He is almost deaf from standing
too close to chainsaws and no longer needs
the money wood brings.

In his wake things look plainer.
Outside the cabin,
smoke makes a feast of air.

The sweater I wear is soft and thick.

SYCAMORE

A hummingbird drinks
unhurried by the cat, its throat afire
in the descending sun.
I meet you and the childhood dove
coos the old owl song, catbirds
twitter, and the world fashions
afternoon out of the cooling air.
The finches do not notice
that the cattails burst with summer.
I would like to be a trellis
that climbs your towering body.

Dreaming in January

Here were the sounds in the world last night:
the winter rain and your breathing.

Nothing new in this. Nothing new ever.
When your breath leaves me, I drive along

the Skalkaho pass to Hamilton,
then on west of Lolo. I hug the lane's instep

and read the humidity flushing out the trees,
the wooden steps, the eave and rail

foresters have left zigzagging the slope.
I will never get that place uncovered

where they released Uncle Bud's ashes
or we fly-fished the lime-green lake

with the broken outboard
and the trout beautiful as day.

The decrepit bridge that crossed the rapids
where the camera fell between the beams—

we took off our clothes to swim
in a pool moraine had cut off from the current

and I was seventeen, the young runoff
stiffening my fingers, tightening my breasts.

You shifted position to favor your bad shoulder.
How many things you can undo.

GOLD DUST

Sometimes in your apartment,
underground, underheated,
with its view of the green gully,
later the shorn, brown gully

and houses closer than we'd imagined,
where we never cooked and rarely ate,
one table covered in letters,
and a side table with a coaster

and one beautiful magazine,
the television on cinder blocks
where basketball often played,
and often silver films,

your home of tenuous shelves
and the bedroom of frames,
whole milk in the refrigerator,
the broken railing to the porchless light,

the daffodil, six tulips and borrowed
trash, recycling, parking,
flimsy chairs and the collected works
of Merrill and Montale,

where old receipts admitted some betrayals
if held under a strangled lamp,
and the paintings seemed
to have been selected

when you were happier,
in that bed whose far end my anklet
was never recovered from,
you read aloud.

Then, in that voice of praise
I saw what I was circling—
something almost proved real,
as one lost in the Sierra Madre

sees how large it all is,
how majesty is the independence
of things from our little striving.
I witnessed it as it ran

through my fingers:
sourceless, unattachable,
sweet.

THE NONCHALANT, THE INFINITE

This street is lit with things you understand,
your Calder whirl and Newman line.

Not my miserly love will ruin and make you.
I can still be saved from some last Pompeii

I see looming: practiced, sad.
Only my appetite for the ocean survives some afternoons.

I have thrown a glass of champagne to the wind
and watched it dance and snake back into the flute.

Then I drank it and a dazzling man poured more,
whispering, *The turtles are hatching in the moonlight.*

After Refusing You, Again

Driving away, the radio asks,
What is the meaning of "slender boy?"
On the road leaves disappear.

Outside the flashlight shows
a shower of maple spotted with disease.
Vermillion disorienting evening.

You are part of the fee exacted
for the folly of trying to describe this.

Part Three

DENDROLOGY

Night rain and wood fire,
winter perch still in the air—

to live on past the Chinese elm
and both the dogwoods

is in at least those ways
no gift. Still,

white birch light some forests.
It was in the Catskills

that my mother first told me
what they were called.

CHARON

The Saudi bracelet I wore from four
to ten finally had to be cut
by a jeweler out of place in the mall
in Hamilton, New Jersey, where he worked.
Not frequent this work, softly
catching the hammered gold
in three fingers, distracting with a question
the way a good nurse inserts a needle.
He understands the gasp, the phantom
against the hand, the strangeness
of placing bracelet in box.
He seems to know how infrequently
the surgeons who ferry us across our rivers
have the gift of knowing what they do.

A WRITING INSTRUCTOR
BEGINS IN THE WORLD

for Richard Bailey

All my friends live in cities.
I wanted to tell someone

where the reddest azaleas are,
convinced again I've found them.

Too late to explain the redbud's arc
or the variations of iris—

their two weeks have passed
and the lilac will not reopen.

Most likely
what I know about these things

cannot be explained,
but what else is worth the trouble?

The echinacea feeds September
its purple

and the cosmos
rescind their tremulous tangle—

I worry that people in cities do not know
that we must love unaccountably.

Coalescence

If plants could love anything,
they would love the roar of rain—
see the rosemary quiver.
But the enthusiasm of plants

is not love. When the ash sways,
sending water everywhere
to consort with the rain,
it is not dance. The droplets

are not candy tossed from a dragon
in a new year's parade.
Still I crave the storm
even as it consumes the porch.

For Helen

Broken moss on the bog where ghosts exhale
their threads to this world on the water's surface.
When the cranberries are red and heavy,
farmers flood the bog and shake them loose.

They float and are skimmed with great combs.

In this way I bring the knots out of my hair
grown almost too long to manage,
I would like a sister in these days to sit behind me
and with her fingers somehow make it right.

I wanted to look into the water cleared of fruit,
a bog or the sink where I've done washing,
where flecks of dirt swirl and settle
like dancers too shy to speak.

I wanted to find evidence of a myth
in my hair grown long, a dark red fruit,
the corolla of some flower whiter than its death.
The gleam of semi-permanence.

We went out in the wooden boat
onto the Great Egg Harbor in the rain
and caught bluefish, stripers, fished
until the camera had its fill,

tossed them back through the air like farewell.

ENKIDU

What you have done in a handful of days with my life
is make it into a necklace
of coins not minted this century.

You spread it across my chest, touching
everything lightly. Sometimes we slept—
remembering it is like reading through

a large jewel. The story is about a kingdom
where lovers drink gold and flourish.

ON ROADS THAT CARS DON'T USE

Walking the county recesses, we found the last
bright maple, counted the purples in the hills.
We listened for the faint snap of snow or evening.
Over an over-vermouthed martini, olives
sour from disuse, you unraveled some of the skein
you keep in your slight body: Brazil, Berlin,
not as many women as might have been, but women.
I want to dwell in the roads of unpicked corn
the crows ignore. A chrysanthemum of gnats hovers
between field and sky, the winter sunset is briefer
than a laugh. You do not squander the apartness
we wander, dishonor your lips with talk.

Six Years On

Probably Atocha still smolders
with good art,
absinthe,

sweet potatoes roasting
in oil drums,
the braille hearts

of flamenco dancers.
I was lit once
with Spain's electric

and stood at the Metro stop
smelling everything
and waiting for you.

The books with their ticket stubs
falling out,
the high heels—

we should have taken pictures
to prove now
that it happened.

Only the world moves.
I stay, crossed by the arctic tern's
grueling going.

ART HISTORY

Everything, down to the old, abandoned Ford,
you inhabited with blue paintings
of antlers, coffee, chains.

You took over
like an abandoned wife
takes over her daughter's life,

you accomplished it
the way fall accomplishes
winter, the way paintings

fall off of walls and the glass breaks
but there he still is, the man in the robe,
holding his side,

and Beatrice walks, and the banjo lesson
is uninterrupted.

CONCERNING GORKY'S
THE ARTIST AND HIS MOTHER

While she gives with one hand . . .
a pigeon disappears.

The painting, its study, the painter
slain, all this
breaks apart naturally.

Piece them together again,
with care for the calico dress,
the child's fist of sweet pea.

How else do you expect
to forget her hat
into which we will vanish?

COCIBOLCA

The world is terrifying
and sometimes you were its terror.
Sometimes, instead, the pool

it could not look into,
where a towel on a branch
and a bar of soap on a rock

were the only clues of anyone
within. More and more
we inhabit a lake.

Pumice stones and catalpa
float in the water,
coke bottles popping open

communicate the shore. The smell of hot
chicken and rice, the stupid gaze
of a skinny, free cow—

and we know we swim in the mouth
of a dead volcano.

OBEISANCE FOR ANCESTORS

Perhaps if we dress in red costumes,
the dead will fear us for another year,
but I think color blindness
is one privilege of ghosts.

I didn't have my own dead, so I adopted.
The house is really filling up.
Each Thanksgiving is a struggle—

so much uneaten squash,
no one able even to locate
cranberries.

Intercessors

for the sculptor Mark Hogencamp

Wars in the world
and the duty to renounce them
with care,

with figures you carve and paint
with nail polish.
The blue-haired one

snaps a neck
and with her gloved hand cupped, says,
Look at what I would do for you.

How to accept all those
we cannot do for:
one man who needs badly

a kiss, another dying
for a good meal.
Too poorly distributed

is the care of the living.
My mother is the saint
of African violets.

And even she is outmatched.

AFTER RYOKAN

Very little wood left
but much more winter—
snow falls in a hush
and trees still damaged
from the last storm wear it.

Even now, as my life stirs
beneath me like a root,
as the beloved fills
the world like a curved screen—
your embers,

quiet. I correct the child
who rushes for water
or yesterday's paper. My house
has room for everyone
as they are.

SAMA'

Hawk swoop, squawk
of magpie, we move west
like morning, like the coastline.

Bring our luck down upon us
to prize each
cloud obscuring the Lake.

I have wandered long enough—
now I ask
to be the beloved of hours

whose path I court,
with the hard wish
to make good.

You see that the earth is a dervish.
Who knows how anybody
stays on it.

Preparing to Leave Virginia

Some things I've known so long
I no longer remember learning them:

lettuce, vinegar and oil make salad.
The Serengeti is in Africa.
Pussy willows are first in spring.

I dream I walk reciting things I know
and deer begin foraging in the clearing.

I mistook their footfall for my neighbor.

They look at me a long time,
being poor judges of danger.

Sometimes what I know is no longer true
and there's no way to tell when

the truth changed or why an airplane
high enough can be the sound of crocuses.

No one should expect to get over
blue mountains.

Hiking the Lake Placid Trail

I was low many times
and I drank the groundwater,

washing my hair
morning and night,
swimming to islands of duck nests.

I wept bitterly at estate sales,
haggling over a nice lamp,
cursing

my own frivolity.
It's all a bunch of junk.
I know a little more than I used to

and I still don't care if you turn out to be
a common thief.

ALEXANDRIA

I wanted to affirm
that all were equally invited
to the world

and my little table in it,
to leave
no bruise upon the grass.

So many failures,
plain as roses
on cloth.

I saw a hummingbird at rest
against the brief coral sky.

His stillness—
how his lungs emptied and filled,
his heart's mad vigil.

Every moment the Galapagos
edge further
towards oblivion.

New islands will come later,
but it's the dying ones
I love.